HOW T

COLORFUL AROMATIC

HEALING CANDLES

Learn to Make Natural

Colorful & Aromatic Candles

At Home

By

Ally Russell

TABLE OF CONTENTS

FOREWORD

Imagine coming home from the stress of the daily grind to the rejuvenating aroma of scented candles in your home, welcoming you to your rest and relaxation. Isn't it simply the most wonderful feeling in the world? Don't you just want to close your eyes, take a deep breath, and cast all of your worries aside?

That's exactly the kind of peace and tranquility that aromatic candles can bring. I should know—I've been nurturing my candle making business for 8 long years, after all. I've successfully sold to different groups of clientele and various markets, and that includes local church events, school events, online via Facebook and other social media channels, local craft stores, and even the flea market.

Business was certainly booming, but on the fifth year mark, I noticed a steady dip in my sales, and couldn't for the life of me understand why. It wasn't until I studied the industry and scrutinized it more did I come to realize that the competition is tough out there and to rise above the cut-throat industry players, I had to adapt; I had to change for the better. That was when I decided to put a little twist into my candle making business, and things were never the same again.

Instead of lowering my price points to match the new players in the niche market, I opted instead to raise my prices. Why you ask? It's because I now knew that my candles had something different, something unique, something more marketable—and that's the fact that my products of love are more aromatic, wrapped in more attractive packaging, and made from all-natural materials—now that's not something you see every day!

It was delightful while it lasted. Sales skyrocketed by 40%, and profits were up by 18%. My buyers were ecstatic about the better quality of candles, and I loved serving them.

Still, nothing truly lasts forever, and all good things eventually come to an end. After a good, full, eight years, I have now decided to retire and travel the country with my husband. I mean, I've even got my own RV to see the world with! And with that notion, I am now opening up and sharing every single thing I know—all the tips and tricks and life hacks and secrets—just so you too can start a lucrative candle making a business of your own.

So, what do you think? Shall we get started then?

TINY BIT OF HISTORY LESSON FOR YOU

Here is a little bit of boring history lesson for you (in case anyone ever asks if you know the history of candle making).

With such a rich and traditional history of being used for birthday celebrations, religious services, holidays, home decorations, and even as the only source of artificial light during the old days, candles used to be made from tallow. This material is extracted from sheep and various cattle during the Roman and early Egyptian times, and while they served their purpose at the time, they burned terribly and were inefficient.

During the Middle Ages, candles began to be made from beeswax for religious and worship purposes, which was indeed a drastic improvement but can be quite expensive in its limited quantity. Candles were thus made available only for the upper class and members of the clergy.

Early settlers in colonial America soon discovered that they could boil berries from the bay-berry shrub and produce a sweet smelling candle, but as the process is tedious and inefficient as well, candle making using this kind of process just wasn't practical. By the 18th century, the rise of the whaling industry gave birth to the widespread availability of whale oil. Whale oil could now be used as a good replacement for tallow, beeswax, and bayberry wax, but the smell of the oil was rather unpleasant.

When the 19th century rolled around, the first patented candle making machines arrived along with braided wicks, as well as new research and discoveries from chemists Michael Eugene Chevreul and Joseph Gay Lussac. Paraffin wax began to be commercially produced—it burned clean and bright and had no unpleasant odor. Cheaper and sturdier candles were then manufactured from paraffin wax and stearic acid.

Today, a wide variety of materials can be used to create candles—beeswax, soy, vegetable waxes, gel waxes, and so much more. In the market today, candles can be broken down into different categories, some of which include the following: container candles are poured into special containers like tan, glass, or pottery.

They are usually for decorative purposes and can have different fragrances added to them. Votive candles are freestanding and usually white and unscented. They are used for gratitude or devotion, usually in religious events and ceremonies.

Taper candles, from their name alone, are very slender and can have heights of up to 20" in total. Tea light candles, on the other hand, are very small and are usually placed in cylindrical aluminum or polycarbonate holders.

There are plenty of colors and fragrances to choose from as well, and we'll get to the nitty-gritty of every single detail in the pages to come. So sit back, put on your thinking cap on, and let's get started.

PART -1

EASY CANDLE MAKING AT HOME

TYPES OF CANDLES

VOTIVE CANDLES

      Votives are poured or molded candles and one of the simplest types of candles to make. They are usually cylindrical or square shaped. Generally, they are about two inches in diameter and two or three inches tall.

They come in this size to fit nicely in standard votive cups. Often, votive candles are used for ceremonies, weddings, memorials, or vigils where people need to hold candles in their hand. Scented votive candles are also used for adding scent to an area.

Pillars are also poured or molded candles and among the easier candle to make. Pillar candles are popular as they are long-burning due to their shape and size; are easy to add scent; and come in sizes from around three inches in diameter to very large, multi-wick size. They are usually cylinder-shaped but are sometimes square.

The simplicity of the pillar allows them to be used in almost any décor from elegant opulence to minimalist modern. Often the style of the pillar is determined by the type of candle holder used. Since pillars are heavy and stable, they can stand alone on just about any flat surface or holder.

MOLDED CANDLES

Molded candles are simple to make by pouring melted wax into any type of mold. Molds come in many different shapes and are often made from glass, metal, plaster, silicone, or acrylic for safety reasons, but you can make molds from many containers you may have around the house such as waxed milk and juice cartons, cans, and muffin cups.

TAPER CANDLES

Tapers are dipped candles that are usually at least six inches tall and up to 14 inches tall. The standard diameter for candle holders for tapers is three-quarters of an inch.

Tapers are displayed in candle holders or candelabras as they cannot stand alone. They are often used as statement pieces for romantic candlelit dinners, weddings, or religious ceremonial displays.

Container candles are excellent candles for soy wax since it does not harden as hard as other waxes because the candle remains in the container and is burned in the container after the wax hardens. Today, the more unique the container for the candle, the more attractive the candle.

Tea light candles are a practical candle used to create a scent when used in essential oil or scented wax diffusers or under chafing dishes to keep food warm until it is served.

Tea lights are also used in decorative candle holders to shine line through a cutout, such as the "window" of a candle holder designed as a winter cabin. To serve these purposes, tealights are shorter than votive candles.

They may be scented if used in essential oil or scented wax diffusers but are unscented when used to keep food warm.

Floating candles are similar to tealights, but they are shaped to float in water while burning for displays.

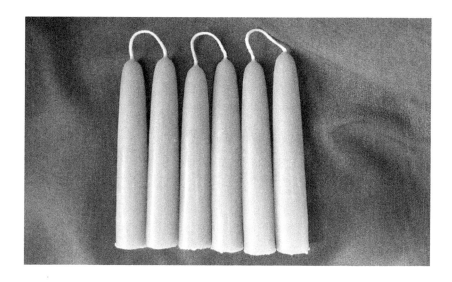

Dipped candles include taper candles and classic birthday cake candles. The candles are formed by dipping the ends of a long wick into melted wax.

The wax-coated wick is then hung over a rack until the wax is cooled and then dipped again until the desired candle size is achieved.

Rolled candles are super easy to create as they are created by rolling a sheet of beeswax tightly around a wick. The beeswax sheets can be rolled into tapers or pillars of varying diameters. Beeswax sheets are available in dyed colors or the natural golden-yellow color.

You may decide to focus on making one type of candle or several types, depending on your personal candle needs and styles or who your targeted market is for your candle business. But do put some thought into what type of candles you will make before you shop for equipment, tools, and supplies.

NATURAL CANDLES VS. NON-NATURAL CANDLES

Because there are tons and tons of guides out there, both online and offline, that teaches you all about candle making, it's important to set yourself apart from all the other industry players out there if you really want to stand out in the market.

Because you want to make your hobby, passion and business as successful and lucrative as possible (who would want their business to fail, right?), you should be able to establish your unique selling proposition right away—and that's by making natural candles with beautiful vibrant colors and aromatic fragrances.

SOY CANDLES

SOY CANDLES VS. PARAFFIN CANDLES

Because paraffin is made from petroleum, this nonrenewable source releases toxic and carcinogenic substances that are harmful to us and the environment when the candle burns. Soy, on the other hand, is made from a natural and renewable source called soybeans, and not only do non-toxic soy candles burn cleaner, but there is also very little soot that is released when the candle burns, keeping those pesky black soot and stains on your furniture and walls down to a minimum.

Soy candles are biodegradable, and they also last longer than their paraffin counterparts because of the slower burning times. The longevity of soy candles is also due to the fact that soybean-based waxes have cooler burning temperatures, allowing you to save up on replacing those candles every so often when they completely burn out.

Soy candles also retain the colors as well as the scents that they are infused with from essential oils. These fragrances are released gradually as the soy candle burns slowly—this also ensures that the scents released into the air are subtle and not immediate and strong.

This natural, sustainable, petro-carbon soot-free, and renewable resource is so much easier to clean up from spills and stains. With just some candle, water, and a hairdryer, you can get those stubborn candles spills off your carpet or furniture as opposed to the dried paraffin wax that takes forever to clean.

They help maintain air quality, can keep your house free from blackened jar tops, soot deposits, and gray residue, and reduce the danger posed by candles to people with asthma, respiratory diseases, little kids, and the elderly. Better yet, whenever you buy soy wax for soy candles, you are also supporting local farmers and helping local agriculture thrive!

CONS OF SOY CANDLES

Of course, not everything is completely perfect when it comes to soy wax candles. Because soy wax has the tendency to contract or to expand, soy candles can be greatly affected by changes in temperature with its natural wax characteristics.

To control this expansion and contraction to some degree, you should consider keeping your soy wax candles in temperatures that are consistently warmer (approximately above 60 degrees) to prevent shrinkage due to colder temperatures and humidity.

Soy wax can also be inflexible with some of the kinds of fragrance oils out there, and you need to remedy this by testing different scent oils before you use them. Always make sure you ask the oil manufacturers how their scented products work with soy wax. With soy candles, you might also have to deal with frost marks in the tart or candle (you can remedy this one by using some soy additives).

Finally, because soy candles are much more natural and safer than paraffin candles, they are usually much more expensive as well. They do burn cleaner and last longer than paraffin candles, so it's a matter of investing in a good and all-natural product and deciding if it is worth the higher price tag.

For your reference, here are some of my recommended brands for choosing and buying your soy wax for your soy candles:

- AAK (formerly Golden Brands) - containers and tea lights
- Ecosoya - pillars, votives, and tarts. You can find Ecosoya in most every candle supply stores including Amazon.

BEESWAX CANDLES

Aside from soy wax for soy candles, another natural alternative in candle making is to use beeswax. Beeswax has long been known throughout the years for its multitude of useful functions and natural characteristics, and because of its many applications in everyday life—which includes arts and crafts, cosmetics, and, of course, candle making—they can be quite practical, with their higher melt point and longevity.

BEESWAX CANDLES VS. PARAFFIN CANDLES

Beeswax Candles	Paraffin Candles
As with anything that is worth the while, beeswax takes a while to produce and is not that easy to create. Bees have to fly approximately 150,000 miles just so that they can collect enough nectar in order to produce an estimate of about six pounds of honey. This is just to secret a single pound of wax; even more difficult and complicated is that a beekeeper can only secure a pound or two of the beeswax for every hundred pounds of honey that is harvested. This is the reason why beeswax is definitely much more expensive than paraffin for candle making.	Paraffin candles are way easier on the wallet, and will definitely not break your budget, paraffin is widely and commercially available, loads cheaper, and makes up an estimate of 95% of the whole candle production industry in the world.
Because beeswax is, as you guessed it, created by bees, it is a hundred percent natural, definitely chemical-	Paraffin contains a myriad of harmful chemical substances that you inhale into your

free, and one of the oldest candle types known to man. Just make sure that when you are buying beeswax candles, always check to see if the ingredients are there. The product should say "100% pure beeswax candles".

poor lungs every time you burn the paraffin candles. Because paraffin is a highly refined oil-based petroleum by-product, it contains benzene, toluene, and a whole lot more toxins.

Beeswax candles burn clean, are environmentally friendly, safe, and non-toxic. They are biodegradable, non-oil based, and does not need to undergo any kind of chemical processing.

Horrifyingly, paraffin candles need to be treated with 100% industrial strength bleach in order to create its black color to white. This manufacturing process alone creates toxic dioxins as by-products—even worse is that the carcinogenic chemical Acrolyn is added to help solidify the paraffin candle. Would you really want to burn these down and willingly inhale them and keep them around in your own home?

This carbon-neutral product has a natural honey scent and floral nectar, creating a pleasant aroma as the candles are burning.

Paraffin candles contain artificial colorants, dyes, and synthetic fragrances that are added and can also produce toxins when burned. Some paraffin candles even contain lead wicks, adding, and even more, environmental damage.

With one of the highest melting points known among waxes, beeswax candles last significantly longer than other candles in the market, with a life longevity of about two to five times more than the average candle.	Paraffin candles burn short, drip too much, and are extremely inefficient. The excessive dripping also produces more toxins and can be quite difficult to clean off.
Beeswax candles can act as natural ionizers because they emit negative ions that help cleanse and purify the atmosphere, improving overall air quality.	Paraffin candles not only release harmful toxic substances that are detrimental to the environment and to overall air quality, but they also leave behind a trail of black soot on surfaces of your house.
Beeswax candles are hypoallergenic and will not aggravate symptoms for those who are suffering from atmospheric sensitivities, asthma, and environmental allergies.	The chemicals that are present in paraffin candles can be extremely harmful to the lungs when inhaled and can aggravate symptoms in kids, the elderly, and anyone suffering from asthma and allergies.

SUPPLIES YOU NEED

Candle making equipment and tools can vary, depending on the type of candles you make, but some basic tools and equipment are necessary for making any type of candles. It's best to gather all your equipment ahead of time and organize it. Doing so ensures that you have everything you need for a successful candle-making session.

Having your supplies and equipment available and organized can also make candle making safer. Candle making requires your focus and presence, so it's not safe to leave the work area during the candle-making process to look for supplies or equipment. Lack of organization in the work area can result in accidents or botched batches of candles. You don't want either!

Since candles are all about the wax and wicks, let's start there. As I said before, the goal of this book is to provide information on natural candles, so the focus is on beeswax and soy wax.

WAX

Of course, when you start any worthwhile endeavor, you need to arm yourself with the right tools and equipment for your so-called battle ahead. Wax is one of the most important supplies you need in your candle making business, and we've spent quite a big part of the beginning of this book talking about the different kinds of natural waxes available to you.

The traditional wax that candle makers have been using since forever is the paraffin wax. It's still the most popular and most widely available commercial wax on the market today, and for a good reason. It's cheap and easily purchasable but contains harmful toxic ingredients and chemicals.

Soy is a natural alternative to paraffin wax, made from soybean oil and is longer lasting, burns cleaner, and is easier to clean. Beeswax is the oldest candle making wax, produced by bees, and is a hundred percent natural. On the plus side, it's totally chemical-free; on the downside, it is also much more expensive and harder to come by.

Soy Wax

Soy wax is a clean-burning, eco-friendly, sustainable wax that is made from the oil of soybeans. Soybean crops are major crops in the United States in Indiana, Illinois, and Iowa. Once the soybeans are harvested, they go through a process of being cleaned, cracked, and hulled.

Then, they are formed into flakes, and the oil is removed from the flakes. To make the oil solid at room temperature, the oil goes through a hydrogenation process that changes some of the fatty acids in the oil from unsaturated to saturated.

There are various types of soy wax. One-hundred percent soy wax is what most people prefer if they are concerned about burning clean candles with no toxic emissions. Pure soy wax is usually used for container candles as the melting point is lower than a soy-blend wax.

Soy wax is known as a one-pour or single-pour wax, meaning it is soft enough that it won't shrink after it is poured into the container and hardens, and therefore, the wax won't release and leave a gap between the container and the candle. When making pillar candles or tapers, often a soy blend wax is used for the benefit of the candle becoming hard enough to stand on its own without a container.

Some soy candle manufacturers claim that soy candles burn 50% longer than candles of the same size made from paraffin, depending on the environment in which they are burned and how they are stored.

Soy wax is white in color and can be purchased in convenient pellet or flake form. When planning the colors of your candles, it's important to realize that soy wax doesn't accept dye as readily as paraffin, and your candles will be lighter in color than if paraffin is used. For instance, it may be difficult to get a deep red or green for winter holiday candles. One of the beauties of soy candles is the softer, natural colors.

BEESWAX

Beeswax can be purchased in various kinds, and the quality of the wax can vary. It's important that you know which beeswax is right for any specific candle-making project. Here are some types of beeswax that you should know.

Brood wax is the lowest quality of beeswax. This is the beeswax that was used in the beehive to house bee larvae.

Because the wax is often left in the beehive for several seasons so the bees don't have to create a new honeycomb before they can lay eggs, the wax becomes darkened from the honey and other stuff that is left behind in it.

When brood wax is used for making candles or other projects, you must first melt it, adding a little water, so the impurities will sink to the bottom of the melting container and can be strained out. Unfortunately, this process causes much of the wax to be wasted.

Capping wax is a commonly used, golden wax for candles. It is fairly clean but should be rendered, without water, before making candles because it may contain bits of bee parts or honey.

Before using, melt the capping wax, and let it sit in the container over a warming candle or other gentle heat source for about an hour while the debris settles at the bottom of the container. Pour the yellow wax on the top into a mold. When it hardens, it's ready to melt for candle-making.

Cleaned yellow beeswax is more expensive than capping wax, but you do not need to render it before using it and, thus, it is usually considered the best type of beeswax for making candles.

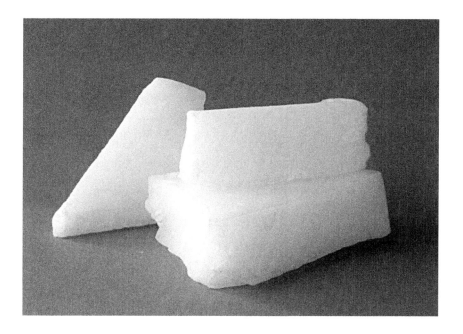

White beeswax is the purest and most expensive type of beeswax as it contains no debris or honey. White beeswax is pure from filtering through a carbon filter, or it is bleached by UV light treatment.

WHERE TO FIND AND BUY BEESWAX

There are various places where beeswax can be purchased, or you can gather your own beeswax if you should decide to keep bees. If keeping bees isn't your thing, but you want "fresh from the hive" beeswax, check with local beekeepers that might have beeswax for sale. You may be able to locate a beekeeper in your area by visiting the American Beekeeping

Federation website: http://www.abfnet.org/ or at *Bee Culture, The Magazine of American Beekeeping* website at http://www.beeculture.com/find-local-beekeeper/

WICK

The size or the width of the wick is the most important factor to consider. Large wicks are usually best for container candles that have a diameter of a few inches. The experienced candle makers know the wick is the most important part of the candle. Even if the candle wax is perfect, the candle will not burn properly without the correct wick.

Wicking for candles comes in various sizes and is often made from cotton, paper, zinc, or wood. The correct type and size of the wicking are based on what type of wax is used for the candle, the diameter of the candle, and the environment in which the candle will be burned (drafty, indoor, or outdoor, etc.).

You need a wick that creates a consistent flame size and a well-formed wax pool without dripping down the side of the candle.

The wick needs to be big enough to draw liquid wax into the flame before it drips down the candle, but small enough to melt only a small pool of wax, so the wick doesn't become flooded with too much wax.

WICKS FOR BEESWAX CANDLES

Finding the right wick for beeswax candles can be a little more difficult than for paraffin wax because there are so many variables in beeswax, such as geographic location, when the wax was harvested, and how it was harvested.

You can follow the general guidelines for beeswax candle wicks but always be aware of the variables in beeswax when making candles, and adjust if necessary.

Candle wicks include the following types: cored, square, and flat wicks.

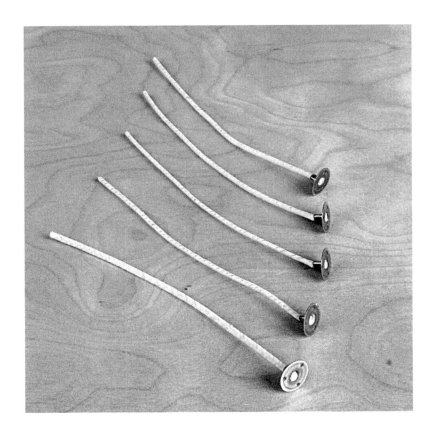

Cored Wicks

Cored wicks have a stiff core made of wire, cotton, or paper. They are often used for votive candles, jar candles, and tea light candles. These wicks are usually purchased already cut to length and with a wick tab attached.

The wick tab is the small round or square-shaped piece of metal found at the end of the wick to help the wick "stand up" in the container. Cored wicks burn hotter so the wax can be completely burned.

SQUARE WICKS

Square wicks are the sturdiest type of wicks and are premium wicks for using with beeswax taper and pillar candles.

FLAT WICKS

Flat wicks are braided with three bundles of fiber and are usually used for paraffin candles but clog easily and are not as suitable for beeswax candles.

The size of the wick must be correct for the diameter of the candle. If the wick is too large, it will smoke as the flame will consume the wax too fast. The candle will also flicker if the wick is too large. If the wick is too small, it cannot burn the wax fast enough, and the wax will pool and drip.

To get just the right size wick, start with a recommended size for the wax type and candle diameter, and conduct tests with different wicks in that size range to see if that is the best size for a specific candle. Sample packages of wicks or small packages of each size are sold by many candle-making suppliers so you can experiment without purchasing large packages of one size.

Every variation can change the way the candle burns and what size wick is needed, including how much fragrance or color is added to the wax and the diameter of the candle container. To test wick sizes, make six of the exact same candles, placing a different size wick in each candle. Label each candle container with the wick size (use a dark marker and write in large print on the label) used for that candle.

Line up the candles on a table or counter and make sure the label is clearly visible or tape an additional note to the table in front of each candle. Light the candles. As they burn, every hour, take a digital photo of the group of candles, making sure you capture the top of each candle so you can check the melt pool.

When the candle has burned one hour for each inch of the candle at its widest point, check the melt pool.

The candle should have a one-half inch melt pool if the wick is the correct size. If the candle has a melt pool smaller than one-half inch, the wick is too small. If the candle has a melt pool that is more than three-fourths inch, the wick is too large.

Cotton Wick Guide

WICK	BURN
UC WICK 1.593 (TEALIGHT)	4.0cm
UC WICK 1.699 (TEALIGHT)	4.3cm
UC WICK 1.300 A	3.3cm
UC WICK 1.375	3.5cm
UC WICK 1.450	3.7cm
UC WICK 1.600	4.1cm
UC WICK 1.651	4.2cm
UC WICK 1.705	4.3cm
UC WICK 1.792	4.6cm
UC WICK 1.832	4.7cm
UC WICK 2.000	5.1cm
UC WICK 2.076	5.3cm
UC WICK 2.164	5.5cm
UC WICK 2.283	5.8cm
UC WICK 2.300	5.8cm
UC WICK 2.402	6.1cm
UC WICK 2.592	6.6cm
UC WICK 2.672	6.8cm
UC WICK 2.775	7.0cm
UC WICK 2.900	7.4cm
UC WICK 2.950	7.5cm
UC WICK 3.000	7.6cm
UC WICK 3.100	7.9cm

Wooden Wick Guide

WICK	BURN
WOODEN WICK SIZE 1	6.5cm to 7.4cm
WOODEN WICK SIZE 2	7.5cm to 8.4cm
WOODEN WICK SIZE 3	8.5cm - 9.4cm
WOODEN WICK SIZE 4	9.5cm -10cm
MORE THAN 10CM	2 WICKS RECOMMENDED

Images source:

https://craftycandlesupplies.com.au/wick_guide_choosi ng_the_best_wicks_for_your_soy_candles/

WOODEN WICKS

Last but not the least, let's not forget the wooden wicks. As customers seek out natural-looking candles, wooden wicks have become quite popular. Some wooden wicks are manufactured in such a way to create a "crackling" sound when burned, like when a fireplace log burns and crackles.

The crackling sound adds to the ambiance of the room.

While wooden wicks are not suitable for beeswax candles, they can be used in soy wax container candles. (Wooden wicks should not be used in votives or pillars.) The recommendation for the wooden wicks size for pure soy candles is the large or extra-large size.

E-Z WICK SETTING TOOL

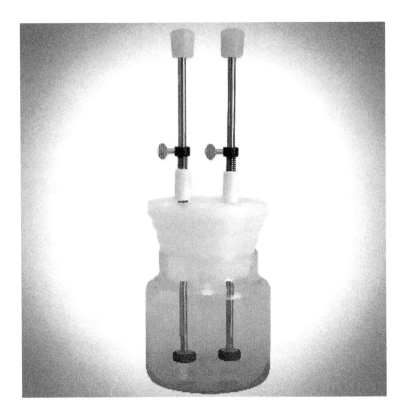

This is an excellent tool that ensures you get perfectly centered wicks in your jars. It works by automatically centering and setting the wick into the container of your choice. The tool works with all possible container sizes.

It is easily adjustable between all various diameter sizes. Though this is not a must-have for making candles, but trust me when I say it will make the experience much easier and fun.

This is all you need to get started with making candles. Next, let's take a look and see what equipment you will need to get started with.

EQUIPMENT GUIDE

DOUBLE BOILER

A double boiler a tool that has one pot inside another little larger pot, you fill up the outer pot with water and inner pot with wax. Once you put it on a stove top, the water warms up, in turn, melts the wax. It is the safest way to melt your wax evenly. A typical double boiler should cost you not more than $40

You can also use a true double boiler or a universal boiler that you can use on top of any of your pots readily available at home. This candle making must keep you from melting the wax directly over your flame source. Make sure that your double boiler can fit in your cupboard as well. As for your containers for the candles, you can use anything from glassware, coffee mugs, mason jars, and anything that you believe can withstand the heat of the candle.

POURING POT

Just as the name implies, the pouring pot is what is used to melt the wax and pour the melted wax into the molds or containers. For the best results, select a pot that is sturdy with an easy-grip handle and pouring spout. Pouring pots range in size, but a good size is a three-quart size that holds about four pounds of wax.

Most pouring pots are made from aluminum and cost between $10 to around $25. Some candle makers prefer to own a pouring pot for each scent they frequently use, so the scent from the previous batch of candles does not transfer to the current batch of wax.

Another useful tool in candle making is the thermometer. This will help you take the temperature of the wax when you're in the middle of your candle recipe—just be sure to follow the instructions in your wax bundle as to which temperature to add fragrance, to pour into your chosen container, and the like.

You can then use a spoon or a spatula to break up wax chunks and stir the wax into an even consistency.

Precision in quantities is essential for consistency in the candles. A good digital or analog scale allows you to weigh ingredients and record the weight of what you used so you can repeat your successes without guesswork.

A digital scale is quick and easy to read, taking the guesswork out of reading the scale accurately. A digital scale is more expensive than an analog scale, but the difference may be made up in fewer mistakes that contribute to the waste of supplies and time.

MOLDS & CONTAINER

Molds come in a variety of shapes and sizes and are made from various materials such as silicone and aluminum. If you enjoy making one-of-a-kind candles, you can create molds out of various household materials such as small waxed juice containers.

The important thing to remember about molds is that you must be able to release the candle from the mold without breaking the candle,

Glass jars of various types are the typical container of choice for container candles when making them in large numbers; however, you can use interesting containers such as small plant pots, tins, small wooden boxes, interesting cups, etc. Be sure whatever container used will not break from the heat of the candle.

Here are some of my recommended stores that you can check out when you are shopping for your candle making tools and equipment, but please understand, I am not anyway associated or an affiliate for any of these businesses.

Also, most online retailers do change often, so at the time you read this, I highly recommend you do your own research on Google and see which online retailers are coming up on top and who is offering the best prices and free shipping.

- Candle Supplies at General Wax & Candle Company
- Bitter Creek Candle Supplies
- Discount Candle Supplies
- MillCreek Soy Wax Candle Supplies
- Nature's Garden Wholesale Candle & Candle Supplies

CANDLE MAKING PROCESS

Typical Candles have four main ingredients

- Wax
- wick
- Color
- Fragrance

SEVEN STEPS TO MAKING CANDLES SUCCESSFULLY AT HOME

STEP 1: MEASURE THE WAX

Here is the general formula that you should follow when you are choosing the amount of wax against your container:

Volume of container in ml X the number of containers X 0.85 = Your Soy Wax in grams

Do not forget to take the lid of your container into consideration. Leave an approximate of about half a centimeter as a gap between the lid and the surface of the wax if your candle container has a lid. Remember that this space will be allotted for your wick so that it can stand when the container is closed!

STEP 2: MELT THE WAX

Use a double boiler to heat the wax to the appropriate temperature. If you need to create a double boiler, you can put about an inch of water in a saucepan and then place the pouring pot in the water. You should add an inexpensive metal trivet or cookie cutter under the pouring pot to elevate it.

When you do this, you will ensure the wax doesn't get direct heat on any side. Then adjust the heat to a medium-low setting. The water needs to boil, but shouldn't be a rolling boil. Water that is at a rolling boil may splatter out of the pan. Occasionally check the temperature of the wax to ensure it isn't getting too hot. Keep adjusting the temperature as needed and never leave the wax unattended.

STEP 3: MEASURE AND ADD FRAGRANCE OIL

Normally, for a soy wax candle, you should add about 6-10% grams of fragrance oil to your soy wax. Here is a general formula for the amount of fragrance oil that you need:

Soy wax in grams X 0.10 = Fragrance Oil in ml

Remember, the fragrance is best measured by weight, but you can also use a tablespoon to measure it if you don't have a scale that measures small amounts precisely. A tablespoon equals 0.5 ounces. Stir the wax after adding the fragrance oil.

STEP 4: MEASURE AND ADD DYE

We will talk more about colors, mixing hues, and the color wheels further on in more detail, but for now, what you need to know is that more wax equals more dye and that you need more dye to achieve darker colors.

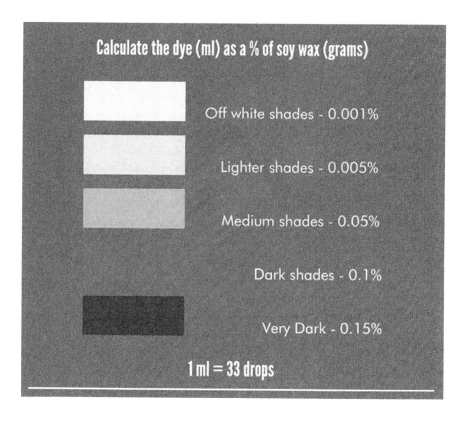

Calculate the dye (ml) as a % of soy wax (grams)

Off white shades - 0.001%

Lighter shades - 0.005%

Medium shades - 0.05%

Dark shades - 0.1%

Very Dark - 0.15%

1 ml = 33 drops

Here is what you need to know regarding calculating how much liquid colored dyes you will need:

Amount of wax in grams X Liquid dye percentage = Liquid Dye Per Candle in ml

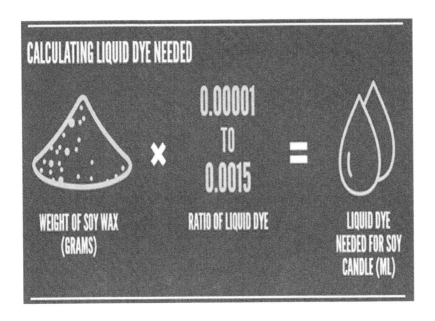

STEP 5: TEST THE COLOR

The liquid wax will often appear darker than once it is completely cooled. To test your coloring, drip a small amount of wax onto a paper plate or towel, being careful not to drip anything on your hands. Allow it to harden, and you can see an adequate representation of what the candle color will look like. If needed you can then add more dye.

STEP 6: ADD UV STABILIZER (OPTIONAL)

This is the time you can add UV Stabilizer if you want. If you choose to add this, you will prevent the color from fading when the candles are exposed to UV rays or fluorescent lighting. You typically add about 1/2 teaspoon per pound of wax.

STEP 7: MIX INGREDIENTS

Remove the pouring pot using something to protect your hand since the handle may have heated up slightly. You may want to set it on some paper towels first to absorb the water from the double boiler. You're now ready to pour your wax.

HOT WAX SAFETY

Before you begin working with wax overheat, you must be aware that each type of wax has a *flashpoint*. The flashpoint of wax is the temperature at which the wax will start to burn and flame.

The flashpoint typically varies from between 250 degrees to 400 degrees, but since the flashpoint is different for various types of wax, it's important that you get the flashpoint information directly from the manufacturer of the wax you are using.

It's also critical that you always use a thermometer when melting the wax. You may be able to "eye it" to some extent, but it's risky not to use a thermometer.

If you do not know the flashpoint for the wax you are using, you are at risk for the wax getting too hot and flaming during the melting process.

This can quickly lead to a major fire in your workspace. (There is more information on wax flashpoints, melt points, and pour points in the chapter on making candles.) Always know the flashpoint and never heat the wax beyond the flashpoint!

If your wax does reach the flashpoint and you have a fire on your hands, *do not use water to extinguish the fire.*

Pouring water on the fire will make the flames soar. Instead of water, use a fire extinguisher to put out the fire. If you do not have a fire extinguisher, though it's recommended that you keep one in the workspace, use sand, baking soda, or flour to put out the flames.

CANDLE MAKING RECIPES

MARBLED CANDLE RECIPE

This is the last variation on the container candle that I want to discuss. This will give you a nice marbled container candle. You can choose to make any color or scent combination you want. It works best with clear containers. When done properly this option gives you a feathered, marbled, nearly tie-dyed appearance. The only additional supply you'll need for this candle is some toothpicks.

Start with the typical container candle process, only make a plain candle with no color. Once you have poured your candle allow it to cool until the wax turns opaque and there's about 1/8 inch of skin on the top of the candle.

This will typically take around 30 to 45 minutes. At this time use a thin wire or a wick pin and push it all the way to the bottom of the container. The more veins of color you want, the more holes you should poke in your candle.

Dab a partial drop of color into the top of each hole. You shouldn't use any less than 1/6th of a drop since a little color will go a long way. Now use a heat gun to heat the top of the candle gently, so the dye will begin to mix with the melted wax. From the outside, you'll start to see the melted, colored wax seeping down along the holes.

Next, you'll want to heat the sides of the jar with even coverage up and down the container. Heat each individual hole for about ten seconds before moving to the next one. The wax on the sides of the candle will melt and combine with the dye to create a swirled or marbled effect.

The convection action of the hot wax will continue even after you stop heating, so don't get too excited about the heating and swirling. About 30 percent of the swirling and marbling will happen after you stop heating the container.

Allow the candle to cool, trim the wick, and you're ready to go with a visually unique candle.

VOTIVE CANDLE RECIPE

These are quick and simple candles to make. You'll need the following supplies:

✓ Candle wax

✓ Fragrance oil

✓ Candle Dye

✓ Wicks

✓ Pouring Pot

✓ Thermometer

✓ Votive Molds

✓ Mold Cleaner

✓ Auto wick pins

✓ UV Stabilizer (optional)

- ✓ Newspaper or butcher paper

- ✓ Paper towels

- ✓ Metal spoon or stir stick

- ✓ Utility knife

- ✓ Wick trimmers, scissors or nail clippers

- ✓ Saucepan

- ✓ Metal Trivet or metal cookie cutter

As with the previous candles, prepare the wax per the instructions. While the wax is melting take the time to prepare your votive molds. Candles work best when poured into clean molds and even if the molds are new they'll have a layer of oil in them from the manufacturing process.

Put a small amount of mold cleaner on a paper towel and wipe the inside of the molds. If you don't have mold cleaner, you can substitute for a Pam type cooking spray. Prepare the wicks in your molds and then arrange your molds in a way that will be easy to pour them.

Add fragrance oil and dye as we've already discussed, making sure you test the color. Add a UV Stabilizer if you want. Mix everything together for three to five minutes. Check the temperature to make sure it is between 165 and 185 degrees. Pour your wax into the molds and fill them completely. Pouring too quickly can cause bubbles to form.

Once the wax has completely settled, you'll likely see a sinkhole that forms when the wax shrinks. Re-melt the leftover wax you should have and allow it to heat to about 190 degrees. The hotter temperature on the second pour will allow it to blend better with the first wax pouring.

The second pour is more difficult. You need to pour the wax so that it is slightly higher than the edge of the mold. Allow the candle to cool completely. Once this happens, you can quickly remove them from the mold by pulling on the wick. If you have trouble removing them you can place them in the freezer for five minutes. However, if you leave them in the freezer too long, then the wax will crack. Trim the wick and place your label, you're ready to go.

PILLAR CANDLE RECIPE

The pillar candle is another simple one to make and is also one of the main candles sold on the market for both decorative and practical purposes. You'll need the following supplies:

- ✓ Pillar Wax

- ✓ Fragrance oil

- ✓ Candle Dye

- ✓ Wicking

- ✓ Pouring Pot

- ✓ Thermometer

- ✓ Candle Molds

- ✓ Mold Cleaner

- ✓ UV Stabilizer (optional)

- ✓ Wick bars

- ✓ Newspaper or butcher paper

- ✓ Paper towels

- ✓ Mold Putty

- ✓ Small screw

- ✓ Cookie sheet or pan

- ✓ Metal spoon or stir stick

- ✓ Skewer

- ✓ Utility knife

- ✓ Wick trimmers or another cutting device

- ✓ Saucepan

- ✓ Metal trivet or metal cookie cutter

As before, prepare your workspace with the newspaper or butcher paper. Measure and melt your wax per instructions. While the wax is melting, prepare your candle molds by cleaning them and putting the wicks in place. Add your fragrance oil and dye to the wax and test your color. Add a UV Stabilizer if you want. Mix everything for three to five minutes and make sure the temperature is between 175 and 185 degrees.

Slowly pour your wax into the mold to avoid bubbles forming on top. Pour until the wax is level with the mold. Once you have filled the mold there will be some wax left in the pouring pot that you'll use later for a second pour, set it aside.

As the wax is starting to set, you need to make a few relief holes. You do this to release air pockets that occur as the wax cools and shrinks. This will prepare your candle for the second wax pouring. Once you see a skin forming on the wax you can use the skewer to poke some relief holes, one on each side of the wick is all you need to do.

You should poke deep into the candle, but avoid hitting the side of the mold. Touching the side of the mold can scar your candle. You also want to make the holes large enough to form a tunnel for your second pour. You need to do this several times as the wax cools. You don't do the second pour until the wax is completely set.

Once you are ready for the second pour, reheat the leftover wax to 185 degrees. Fill the holes to make the second pour level with the first pour. If you go past the level of the first pour, you will develop a seam line in the final candle.

After the second pour has completely set, you can remove the candle from the mold. Remove the putty and the screw from the bottom of the mold and gently slide it off the candle. If you have trouble removing the mold you can freeze it for five minutes.

If you use the wick to help you remove the candle make sure you don't pull too hard to prevent breaking the wick or causing it to come out of the candle. Trim the wick and attach your label or other packaging and you're ready to go.

BEESWAX HAND-DIPPED CANDLE RECIPE

Beautiful hand-dipped candles are easy to make on days when you have plenty of time on your hands. Though they are a bit time-intensive, the result is worth the effort. Using this method for creating hand-dipped candles, you can make candles of the size of your choice.

Supplies You Need

- Cleaned yellow beeswax

- Wicking that is cut into appropriate lengths
- Covering to protect floor, countertops, and tables from drips
- Wax Pot
- Deep pot for melting wax
- Candy thermometer for testing wax temperature
- Rack for drying candles (This can be dowel rods, spring-tension rods, or PVC pipes placed firmly between two sturdy structures (such as doorway), or you can use a wooden drying rack.

Process

- Cover the floor and surface tops of your workspace with a drop cloth or layers of newspaper.
  - Put water in the deep pot so that it reaches about halfway to the top of your melting pot. Put on stove over medium heat.

  - Fill the melting pot with cleaned yellow beeswax.

  - Allow the beeswax to melt slowly. Do not become impatient and turn up the heat and risk damaging the wax. Do not leave the room while the beeswax is melting. The melting could take a few hours so be prepared to do something else in the same work area while the dipping wax is melting.

- Cut the wicks to two inches longer than the length of the candle you are making. The V of the wick should be upright on the wick.

- If you are making pairs of tapers and want the tapers the exact same length, tie two wicks in the upright direction at the top. It's not recommended to use one long wick folded over for two candles.

- When the beeswax begins to melt, prime the wick by dipping it into the wax three or four times, so the wax saturates the wick. Straighten the wick, so it is not curved at all, by holding the top of the wick and pulling on the bottom of the wick simultaneously.

- Keep the wick straight when you dip it until enough wax has adhered to the wick to weigh down the wick and keep it straight. It can be useful to use a skewer or pencil to do this task.

- Dip the wick into the wax. Hold the wax-coated wick up, but over the melting pot, until the dripping stops. Dip again. Repeat the process until the candle is of the desired diameter. (Note: if you dip the wick several times and do not see a build-up of wax, your wax may be too hot. In this case, lower the temperature of the wax by about five degrees and try again.)

- Between dips, after the last dip has stopped dripping, roll the candle gently on a hard, cool surface (marble works great!) to help the candle retain a uniform shape.

SOY TEA LIGHT CANDLE RECIPE

Just as a brief overview, you can make tea light candles and start your candle making a business from here. Making natural tea light candles is easy, simple, and can be colored or scented however way you want to!

Materials:
- A quarter pound of soy wax
- Candle and candle scale

- 1/4 oz. fragrance oil
- 1 drop liquid dye (orange color)
- 8 Tea light cups (clear)
- 8 ECO 0.75 pre-tabbed wick
- A pouring pitcher
- Double boiler
- Hotplate (in the absence of a double boiler)
- Thermometer
- Metal stirrer or wood stirrer

Directions:

Put the quarter pound of soy wax in your small pouring pitcher. Then, heat this container to approximately 185 degrees with your double boiler or your hot plate. Be sure to observe while the wax is melting, and while you are waiting, you can start prepping your tea light cups. Place one ECO 0.75 pre-tabbed wick right in the center of every clear plastic tea light cup (take note that there should be four plastic prongs on the bottom to help guide you when you are trying to center your wick into the right place).

At this point, the soy wax will have reached 185 degrees, and you can now add in a drop of your liquid dye. For about 2 minutes, keep stirring gently and thoroughly to mix the color well. Remove from the heat afterward, and pour in your fragrance oil, constantly stirring.

Let the wax sit and allow it to cool to about 135 degrees. Then, you can now pour in the wax into your prepped tea light cups. Make sure that as you pour the wax in, there won't be any air bubbles forming inside. Also make sure that the wicks are straight and centered in every cup, just to ensure that the burning is safe. Then, let the tea light candles cure overnight, and enjoy! Now, wasn't that just easy-peasy?

HOW TO MAKE SOY CANDLES IN THE MICROWAVE

If you don't have a double boiler or a hot plate at home, you can also make your candles in the microwave to get you started as you experiment with the various methods, scents, and colors of your candles. It's quick, easy, and convenient!

Materials:
- Golden Brands 464 Soy Wax 10 lb Bag
- Fragrance or essential oil
- 8 oz. candle tins

- ECO 14 6" Pre tabbed Wick
- Three-wick bars
- A scale for weighing your wax
- 4-6 Cup Microwave Safe Container – You can also reuse this for candle making; just be sure you do not reuse it with food.
- Microwave – Of course, this is the point of the recipe after all!

Directions:

First of all, always make sure that your container is safe to use for the microwave. You wouldn't want to start a fire or ruin some perfectly good household appliances while you are making your natural candles. Place these microwave-safe containers in the scale, and weigh 16oz. of soy wax.

In the microwave, heat your wax for about 5 minutes on high. Remember that actual heating times can always vary depending on the microwave model and settings, so observe your wax as it is heating and adjust accordingly.

When the designated 5 minutes (or however long it may take depending on your microwave) is up, remove the hot container of wax (very carefully and don't burn yourself!). Check to see if the wax is completely melted; if it is not, stir it for a bit, and pop it right back into the microwave and keep heating in 30-second intervals until you are sure that the wax is melted completely.

When you are happy with the melted consistency of your wax, add in about an ounce of your fragrance oil into your wax. Stir this in constantly and let the wax cool while stirring for about 2 minutes.

When the wax is good and cooled, you can now start prepping the tins. Pour in the wax into your candle tins carefully, making sure that the wick is at the center of the tin. You can do this by using a wick bar just to be sure that the wick is nice and centered.

Let the candles harden and cool overnight, then remove the wick bar. You can then trim the wick to about 1/4 of an inch. To be completely safe, make sure that you let your candle cure for at least a whole day before you light it up and burn it. And there you go!

PART - 2

COLORING BASICS FOR YOUR CANDLES

UNDERSTANDING AND USING COLORS TO ENHANCE YOUR CANDLES

COLOR IN OUR LIFE

Whether you are looking at colors from a spiritual outlook or simply a material stance, different shades and tones reflect some sort of meaning in our lives. For the color red, it usually evokes feelings of strong passion, love, or even anger and war. It can be aggressive, stimulating, and exudes an aura of importance. It is a dominating color and adds gravity, awareness, and demands attention. Orange is playful, energetic, and can add excitement without being too intense.

It can also suggest health and vitality, as well as youthfulness to some extent. As for the color yellow, it is happy, friendly, revitalizing, and summery. It signifies the brightness of the sun, and can often evoke positive light feelings of summer fun. If you want to portray elegance and antiquity, however, simply turn yellow into a darker shade such as gold, and you are good to go.

Green almost always refers to foliage, nature, and prosperity. It evokes elements that are natural, cleansing, organic, and represents the environment. It can create an outdoors feeling, and because it is almost like a bridge that connects the warmer colors of red, orange and yellow to the cool colors of blue and purple, green tends to be the most balanced color that stands out softly against other hues.

The ever-popular color of blue signifies trust, calm, serenity, and peace. It is a cool color that is friendly and inviting and is often even relaxing. It can call to mind memories of the sea, with the vibrancy of water and the sky. Darker shades of blue can signify professionalism but bear in mind that the color blue itself can be quite an appetite suppressant.

Purple shows off wealth, luxury, mystery, and romance. It is associated with decadence, elegance, or a high-end appeal, and can be quite sensual in darker tones and shades. Pink can also be romantic, but it evokes a soft mood that's young, innocent, and feminine. It can also be a sugary sweet connotation, which helps customers reminisce about childhood and carefree youth.

Brown has always been related to earthy, rustic, and natural tones. It is usually maximized with green to give off an outdoorsy vibe that reminds of earth and trees. Black is powerful, mysterious, edgy, and sophisticated. It gives off a no-nonsense air of elegance as well and is bold and simple. It might also signify death and mourning. White, on the other hand, is one of the most common candles out there. It is clean, simple, pure, and fuss-free.

As individuals certain colors speak to us, in what we find comforting, energizing, or allegorical to our aura/ personality. The colors and scents we add to candles can make all the difference in how they visually appeal to you and your customers and/ or friends. Unlike store- bought candles, you have the option to personalize and style your own candles in a more attractive and indulgent design.

UNDERSTANDING THE COLOR BASICS

There are three primary colors of which every color of the rainbow and under the sun are made of. These colors are magenta, yellow, and cyan: or more typically referred to as red, blue, and yellow. When mixed together in small doses, you can create any color you can imagine!

Thus, producing the color wheel. A color wheel is a basic tool that is referenced when combining colors and was first originated by Sir Isaac Newton in 1666. The wheel was designed to that essentially any colors you choose from the circle will look great together.

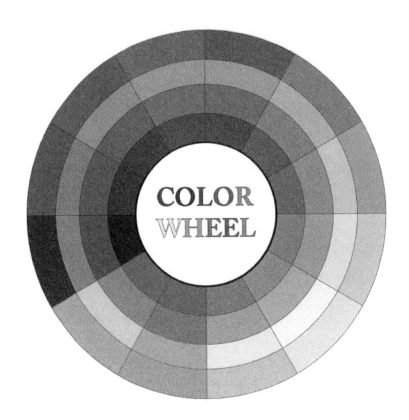

(Color wheel)

Obviously, the wheel has changed slightly over time, but the fundamental version of it features twelve colors. There are traditional color combinations that are naturally alluring when paired together: these are color harmonies or chords. This is when two or more colors have a specific relation to one another on the color wheel.

(Primary Colors)

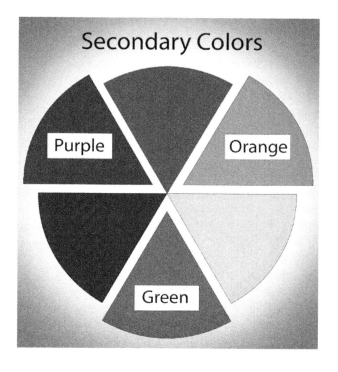

(Secondary Colors)

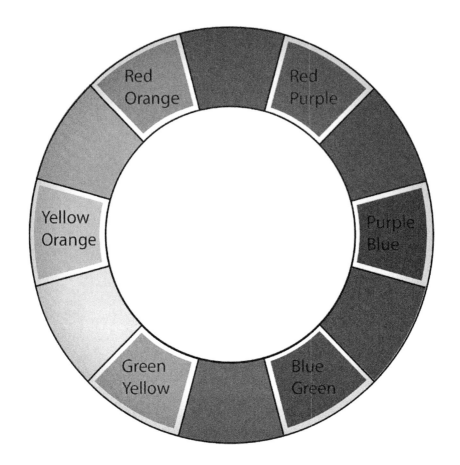

(Tertiary Colors)

PRIMARY, SECONDARY, AND TERTIARY COLORS

Like I said before, the primary colors on a color wheel are red, yellow, and blue. Then come the secondary colors: green, orange, and purple.

Blue + Yellow = Green

Red + Yellow = Orange

Red + Blue = Purple

Lastly, there are six tertiary colors that can be produced by simply combining the primary colors with the secondary colors. The six tertiary colors are red-orange, yellow-orange, yellow-green, blue-green, blue-violet, and red-violet.

Red + Orange = Red- Orange

Yellow + Orange = Yellow- Orange

Yellow + Green = Yellow- Green

Blue + Green = Blue- Green

Blue + Purple = Blue- Violet

Red + Purple = Red- Violet

Even though there are only seven colors of the rainbow, the spectrum of shades, tints, and overall variety of mixed colors are endless. You may be thinking that all you need to do to the color candle is simply throw some dye into your batch and get the exact color you had in mind for your candle.

You can get the perfect shade of pink or a natural green tone to bring your ideal color into manifestation for your homemade cleanser. But, it does take a bit more time, precision of ingredients, and thoughtfulness to make it happen.

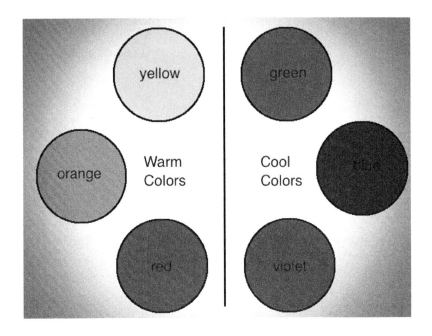

(Warm vs. Cool Colors)

Colors are categorized into two subsections: warm and cool. Warm colors are intense, energetic, vibrant, and associated with heightened emotions. Think of a vivid orange or passionate, rich red. Other examples of warm colors include red- violet, yellows, browns, oranges, and reds. Cool colors evoke a sense of calm, relaxation, and are soothing to look at. Cool colors are often associated with nature and meditation;

like a bright forest green or beautiful ocean blue. Cool colors are comprised of purples, blues, and greens.

Now you might be wondering, "Can colors actually make you feel hotter or colder?" The answer is absolutely! Warm and cool colors can also make a room seem brighter or darker. If you live in a climate that is mostly hot throughout the year, you may decorate your house with cooler color schemes, so the heat feels less overwhelming. The opposite is also true and often practiced.

Lodges and hotels that are close to ski resorts and other winter getaways are usually decorated with reds, browns, and other deeper and deeper colors to evoke a sense of warmth and hominess. All this information may not appear to relate directly to the candle and how to make your own. But the effect that color can have your vision can make the difference in how your homemade creation will make you feel or appeal to the customer if you choose to sell your candles.

USING A COLOR WHEEL TO CREATE SCHEMES FOR YOUR CANDLES

When you are trying to use varying colors for a single candle, it is best to use complementary colors or colors that are analogous. This means that it is best to use the colors that are next to each other on the color wheel if you are going for an analogous look, and colors that are opposite each other on the color wheel for complementary colors.

Because colors have also been known to evoke certain feelings and emotions in people, you might also want to take advantage of this kind of effect when you are trying to sell your colorful candles to your customers.

Regardless of any craft or project, if it is candles or candle, you want to create a beautiful and evoking visual presentation that will mean something to you or the person you make the product for.

A great way to package a gorgeous blend of colored cleansers is to understand and efficiently use complementary, analogous, triadic, split- complementary, and rectangular color schemes to generate a sense of color harmonies.

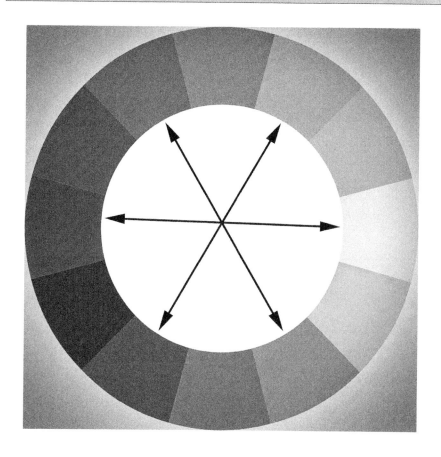

(Complementary Color Wheel)

Complementary colors are on the opposite sides of the color wheel from each other. For example: red and green, or yellow and purple. Using complementary colors creates a vivid and highly energetic look, especially when paired at full saturation.

When continuously used for one project, these colors can be challenging due to their vibrancy. However, in small doses and appropriate spaces, complementary colors are perfect for making your candle stand out.

ANALOGOUS COLORS

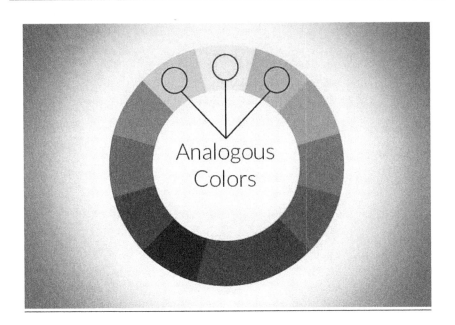

(Analogous Color Wheel)

Analogous colors are right next to one another on the color wheel. Color schemes that feature analogous colors are typically cohesive and form truly serene and pleasant designs. These colors are harmonious and usually very organic, but can also not offer enough contrast.

When using analogous colors with making your candle, choose one shade that will dominate the visual effect and a second that will support or complement it.

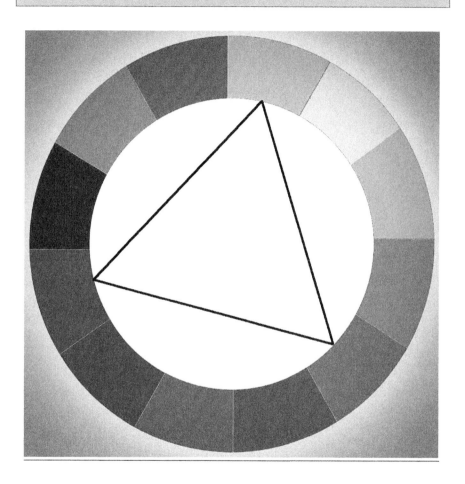

(Triadic Colors)

Triadic colors are recognized by their even spacing around the color wheel. Color schemes that primarily utilize triadic colors are naturally harmonious and well balanced. Triadic colors are comprised of three individual colors that are vibrant together even when undersaturated.

While making candle bars, allow one color to dominate the visual appeal and the other two to create a congenial accent.

SPLIT- COMPLEMENTARY

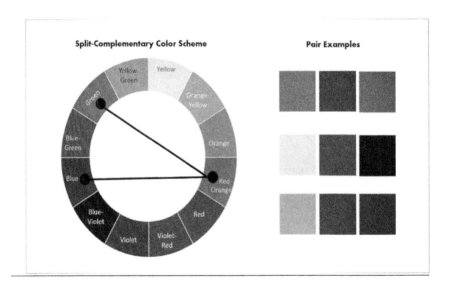

(Split-Complementary Color Scheme)

A split- complementary color scheme is similar to a normal complementary color arrangement but uses two adjacent colors to highlight a base pigment.

Split- complementary creates a strong contrast with less tension than typical complement colors, simply by adding a third color into the mix.

RECTANGLE COLORS

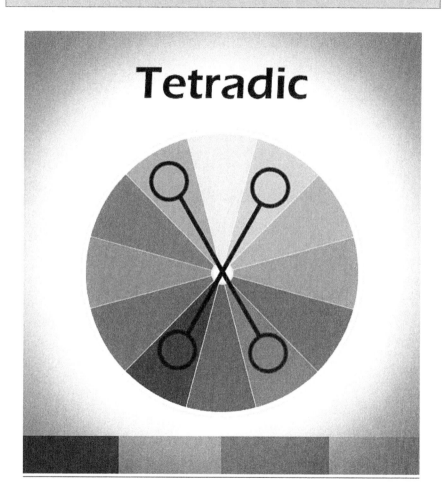

(Tetradic Colors)

A rectangle or tetradic color scheme is exactly what it sounds like! This scheme uses four colors by utilizing two complementary combinations.

Tetradic color schemes are rich and full of many variations and possibilities that can create dazzling designs for your candles! Rectangle color schemes are best used when allowing one color to be dominant.

COLORING TECHNIQUES

When you are mixing your colors for creating your candles, one of the biggest issues you will encounter is uniformity of colors in every batch. It's definitely a big turn-off for customers to see a batch of candles lined up against one another in shelves and seeing that their colors are slightly different from each other.

Especially when you are making your candles for wholesale purposes, the best way to solve this problem is to make larger batches. Increasing your batch sizes helps you measure your dye more accurately, and you can do this simply by using a bigger melt tank—this is the only way to simulate producing the perfect "factory" candles despite the big investment.

When you measure your color, it is essential to be consistent with your tools and to use high-quality ones to produce the best results. Your scale, measuring cup, or dropper need to be precise every single time.

To make sure that each drop is consistent with your previous one, you can try to put a few drops onto a white heat-resistant surface so that you can have a visual comparison of the consistency of each drop of color.

If you are really not able to keep your colors uniform and consistent, the best you can do is to inform your customers beforehand. For online purchases, for instance, customers can take into consideration that monitor settings and color preferences might not show the exact same colors as the actual products.

In any case, you can add a little disclaimer that says that actual colors may vary. After all, customer satisfaction is key to any thriving business, and having a customer complain about poor color choice is one surefire way to hurt your ratings.

Some additional tips and tricks to keep in mind:

- Natural dyes can come in powder form, liquid form, chips, and flakes.
- Oil-soluble dyes can easily mix with waxes, but pigments may be more difficult to dissolve. Yes, pigments do add richness and color depth, but they are not easily soluble. Colorants that are not dissolved well might cause speckles, fading, bleeding, and wick clogging.
- Mixing your dye with fragrances will help increase the solubility of your liquid or powder, which we will talk about in further detail in the fragrance section.

MIXING COLORS

Now that you know the basics and techniques in color mixing, it's time for you to know which colors mix well with each other and which colors will yield which hues. Here is just a simple list of the possible color combinations you can use; but as with anything, remember that you can always mix and match colors on your own.

Don't be afraid to experiment and have fun—who knows? You might even create a whole new color that's uniquely yours alone!

- Blue - primary color
- Yellow - primary color
- Red - primary color
- Black – Black is not a color that you can make on your own. In order to produce the black color, you need to add in some dyes and liquid or powdered dyes.
- White – Simply do not add any color to make white candles.
- Orange – Mix in some yellow and red.
- Pink – Use red but do so in smaller quantities for the lighter pink color.

- Ivory – Add in a little bit of brown to your white candle.
- Burgundy – Use the red color and add in a small quantity of black.
- Brown – Mix in some yellow, blue, and red.
- Plum or Purple – Mix in some blue and red.
- Teal – Use blue with a little bit of yellow.
- Green – Mix in yellow and blue.
- Cinnamon – Use brown and add in a little bit of red.
- Sage – Use green and add in a little bit of brown.
- Navy Blue – Use blue and add in a little bit of black.
- Fuchsia – Use red and add in a little bit of blue.
- Peach – Use orange in smaller quantities.

HOW TO MAKE NATURAL COLORS

Because we are all about all things natural and chemical-free in this book, I will be teaching you how to make your own natural colors for dying your candles, of course! Natural items like turmeric, plant or dying material, and other spices have always been traditionally used for making natural dyes. You can place these ingredients in a coffee filter sachet or a cheesecloth and create your own tea bag type of dye to prevent any unwanted mess when infusing with your hot wax.

Spices are a bit of a two-in-one ingredient because using them for your natural dye will not only create beautiful colors for you but will also help you create aromatherapy candles that are soothing and rejuvenating. Ground spices in the form of powders will help produce pigments, such as orange colors for turmeric and sassafras.

- <u>Cinnamon</u>: cinnamon will give candles a rich brown color.

- <u>Cloves</u>: will create a beautiful rich dark brown.

- <u>Paprika</u>: This spice will create a delightful, vibrant orange.

HERBS

Herbs were the original synthetic dyes, and when herbs are heated in oil, you can extract their colors and add them to the hot wax. Of course, you will need to strain out the plant parts of the herb before you go ahead and dip your candles.

These herbal dyes can produce a light and summery yellow color with wild celery, a deep and elegant purple with sunflower seeds, vibrant orange with ground lichen, and beautiful blue colors with elderberries. You can also create passionate red colors with dandelions and St. John's wort.

PLANTS

- Alfalfa: Use dried and ground alfalfa to create a medium green.
- Calendula: These will make beautiful yellow streaks in your Candles.
- Carrots: Use this to design a yellow-orange color.
- Chamomile: This will give a beautiful beige- yellow.
- Chlorophyll: Powder chlorophyll will give you a beautiful natural green color.
- Green Tea: Green tea powder will make candles brownish green.
- Henna: Henna dye will help your candles turn a deep olive- brown-green.
- Indigo: This plant will create a dark rich blue, but will easily stain your clothes and fingertips!
- Sage: Using ground sage will produce a rich greenish brown.
- Wheat Grass Juice: This natural dye will give your candles a bright organic green color

Because lots of flower petals contain natural dyes, you can add them into your hot wax to yield a variety of different textures and colored dyes. To make brown colors, you can use coneflower and goldenrod. For red colors, you can use dried hibiscus flowers, roses and lavender for pink colors, and cornflower and hyacinth for blue colors.

Quite amazingly, you can create green colors with snapdragons and foxglove, reddish purple colors with day lilies and safflowers, and peach hues with Virginia creepers. Because you can easily see and almost predict the kind of color that a flower might produce, you can go ahead and play with these hues on your own and see where the colors take you!

- Pink Rose Clay: As the name suggests, pink rose clay will make candles brownish- pink.
- Rose Hips: This accessory fruit creates a burgundy brown color, and is high in vitamin C.
- Safflower and Saffron: Safflower petals and saffron root will turn your candles yellow to orange.

If a few pieces of fruit get smashed somewhere along the way from the supermarket to your home, don't fret. You can use mashed fruit to create beautiful and lively colors in candles, because why should you waste some perfectly good fruit? Because fruits like blueberries contain natural dyes (hence the finger stains when you're deliciously munching on them to your heart's delight), you can use artichokes for green colors and huckleberries for purple/reddish hues.

For instance, you can use cherries, strawberries, and raspberries for pink shades, and blackberries and elderberries for the purple and blue hues. You can even use beetroot to create dark brown colors and onion skins for orange. Who would have thought?

- Annatto: When infused in oil, annatto create a yellow-orange color.

- Black Walnut: Ground black walnut will produce purple and black specks in your candles.

- Poppy Seeds: Poppy seeds will add black specks for an appealing design

- <u>Moroccan Red Clay Powder</u>: This ingredient will dye your candle brick red.

- <u>Pumice</u>: Pumice is a type of volcanic rock that will turn candle grey.

- <u>Sandalwood</u>: Sandalwood powder will sometimes turn your candle red-ish brown, and other time it will become light yellow.

- <u>Spirulina</u>: This alga will create a blue-ish ocean green color.

- <u>Wood Powder</u>: This ingredient will produce beautiful shades of blue.

EXTRACTING NATURAL COLORS FROM PLANTS, SEEDS, AND FLOWERS

Take note, though, that some flowers, herbs, and botanicals can clog your wick when you add them to candles for that much-needed color (note that using crayons can also clog your wick, and can even cause smoking). To solve that clogging issue, use a simple oil infusion technique.

Place some of your soy wax or natural wax in a double boiler. Melt it, then place the herbs in a tea bag or coffee filter that's heat sealable, and tie the bag with a string. Afterward, put the herbal bag or filter into your pot of wax. Keep steeping over low heat, and eventually, you will see that the color of your herb will begin to tint the wax (this can actually take a few hours, so just be patient—anything worth the while takes time!).

If you want, you can also place the wax and herbs in a bowl, and set this bowl in a crock pot water bath, keeping the temperature low. When it's done, you can add this tinted wax to your candle mixture, and you'll get the colors you desire!

Here are just some of the botanicals that you can use for this infusion method:

BLUES

- Indigo
- Poppy Seeds
- Blue Chamomile Oil
- Blue Cornmeal
- Woad Powder

BROWNS

- Cilantro
- Ginger
- Rose Petals
- Cocoa
- Cloves
- Cinnamon
- Coffee Grounds
- Rosehips
- Dead Sea Mud

GREENS

- Alfalfa
- Aloe Vera
- Fennel

- Cucumber
- Hill
- Wheatgrass
- Spirulina
- Spinach
- Sage
- Seaweed
- Henna
- Rosemary Powder

ORANGES

- Pumpkin
- Carrots
- Safflower
- Orange Juice

YELLOW

- Saffron
- Ground Calendula
- Blueberry
- Cornmeal
- Blackberry
- Marigolds

- Curry
- Turmeric
- Chamomile
- Orange Peel
- Dandelions

PART – 3

ADDING NATURAL FRAGRANCE TO YOUR CANDLES

SCENTING YOUR CANDLES WITH ESSENTIAL OILS

Now that you have finished learning how to color delightful and charming homemade candles, you are ready to learn how to scent them! The most common method of scenting candles is essential oils. You will have a difficult time finding other suitable ingredients that will scent your candles with a strong, lasting fragrance.

Essential oils are derived from plants through a process known as 'distillation.' Distillation is generally done with steam or water, with as many parts of the plant as possible: i.e., the stems, petals, roots, barks, and leaves. Once the distillation process is complete, the resulting liquid is a highly- concentrated part of what makes an essential oil.

Essential oils carry the characteristic elements of fragrance and additional benefits that are typically found in the plant itself. The properties that are extracted that are in the essential oil contain the true or pure essence of the plant.

Some of the additional benefits include a wide range of healing capabilities. While the natural coloring agents and oils offer a variety of health benefits, essential oils bring a third layer of natural healing.

A common misconception about essential oils is that they are the same as perfume or fragrance oils. While fragrances and perfumes are artificially made in a lab, essential oils are completely natural and organic.

Human-made fragrances are crafted to impersonate natural smells that have a slightly synthetic linger, but they do not offer the natural medicinal benefits that true essential oils are equipped with. However, only completely pure essential oils can be utilized for aromatherapy practices.

I began using essential oils immediately in both my candle and soap making, as I realized that the coloring ingredients did not always hold a strong smell when integrated into candle batter.

There are dozens of scents to choose from, and each one offers different benefits. When combining oils, you can make a candle that is equipped to fend off most illnesses and ailments! However, there are a few words of caution that come with crafting with essential oils. If after reading this chapter you do not feel comfortable handling the oils, you can use fragrance oils instead.

WHAT ARE ESSENTIAL OILS USED FOR?

Believe it or not, essential oils have been a prominent and common holistic tool for cultures and nations around the globe. You have most likely heard a bit about the benefits that diffused essential oils, or pure oils have to offer.

When still inside a plant, essential oils provide protection against life-threatening disease and other predatorial elements, as well as aid in the process of pollination.

The discovery of these benefits for the plant-inspired ancient medical practitioners to utilize the oils for healing practices. Although essential oils are categorized as holistic remedies by the modern science-driven health industry, the trend of using oils for everyday purposes has increased dramatically over the last few years.

Now, therapists and experienced herbal practitioners are encouraging patients to treat psychological and physical disorders with essential oils.

When I first started investigating the benefits of essential oils, I had no idea what I was in for. There are hundreds of articles online and books available that all gave me so much information, it was difficult for me to keep up with the knowledge I was being presented with.

What I came to find was that essential oils have had an incredible historical impact on medicine and truly do make a difference to your physical and mental health. The most common practice of essential oils is for therapeutic purposes, via aromatherapy.

Whether or not you believe in spirituality, oils are thought to have a powerful, uplifting impact on a person's mind and spirit. Each oil offers some sort of aid to threatening ailments and infections, which can bring your homemade candle to the next level!

For example, lavender is known to relieve stress, anxiety, and depression. It is also great for alleviating mental fatigue, panic attacks, bruises and stretch marks. Peppermint essential oil will help relieve nausea, dizziness, and headaches.

Even more miraculous is the effect that frankincense has on your physical health: stimulating your immune system, alleviating asthma, and treating bronchitis. Later on, we will explore and classify more essential oils that can bring life and energy to your candles.

METHODS OF SCENTING YOUR CANDLES

Fragrance oils are not usually utilized for aromatherapy, but they do help give your candles that naturally delightful scent. You can use anything from your favorite flowers to pine cones, fir cones, and needles, or anything from roots to leaves to barks. You can make use of citrus rinds, tree sap, or even hardened resin—basically anything in nature around you depending on where you live.

Make sure that your plant material is well-dried, and simply crush and cover them with oil and stir in over the heat. This usually takes about six hours or so, because plants need to simmer for a relatively long time before they release their aromatic oils.

You can melt your wax or vegetable shortening with a pouring temperature of 180 F (82 Celsius). Add your plant material to your wax, and leave it on the stove for about forty-five minutes, making sure that you keep the temperature at 180 F. When the mixture cools off, strain the wax in its liquid form into a clean glass or your candle jar. Just be careful not to burn yourself!

OTHER METHODS OF SCENTING

When you want to use candles to stimulate the senses or restore balance to your mind, body, and soul, you can use these other methods of scenting, depending on whatever is most convenient for you.

WAX BEADS

Using wax beads is one of the most mess-free options in scenting your candles. These wax beads are usually larger than sand granules, and they can come in a variety of colors. To begin, gather your glass jar or container, your wick, and the fragrance essential oil that you want.

Hold the wick in the center of your jar, then simply pour the wax beads inside. Remember to leave approximately an inch of space at the top of your wick above the wax beads. Then, flatten and smooth the beads using a spoon, making sure that the beads are evenly distributed.

Drop in your fragrance oil with a dropper with about 3 to 4 drops for a light scent (just add more drops if you want the scent to be stronger). With a toothpick, you can stir the beads slowly so that your fragrance oil can seep in throughout the container. Let the wax absorb the oil by giving it some time to settle, which is about a day or two. Then, light it up and enjoy!

HERBAL CANDLES

Heat your wax to about 180°F (this is the usual pouring temperature for most waxes), then infuse your fresh herbs into the melted wax. You can use strongly scented herbs such as lavender, rosemary, lemon verbena, and the like. Keep this temperature up for about forty-five minutes, then strain the wax.

Remember to soak your wick in a small amount of your essential oil first before you place it into the mold. Afterward, add in a few drops of your essential oils—about a quarter of a teaspoon for a single pound of wax—and stir well to distribute the fragrance and prevent any discoloration spots.

Keep in mind that fragrance, when exposed to air, will dissipate, so it is best to store your scented candle in a closed container to prolong the fragrance for a long time.

When you are scenting your candles using herbal ingredients, it is also good to take note of the color of your candles at the same time. For instance, it might be a tad bit off-putting to smell a vanilla scent from a green or black candle, so make sure that the appropriate scent is matched to an appropriate color if you don't want to turn off your customers with jarring combinations.

Some natural candle waxes, unlike paraffin, are not completely scentless. Beeswax, for example, has a natural honey scent all on its own, so it's best if you take into consideration the wax's natural scent before you add in scents of your own.

Always take note of complementary scents and fragrances so that you do not make the mistake of creating pungent smells for your next future batches.

ESSENTIAL OILS

Extracted by steam distillation, essential oils are fragrances that are directly derived from the natural sources. They usually do not have additional chemicals and additives compared to fragrance oils, but they can sometimes be difficult to work with because they tend to have natural reactive properties against some candles and waxes.

As with anything, before you make any large purchases, always make sure to try out some samples sizes so that you can see if your waxes and essential oils are compatible with each other.

Plants that yield essential oils make use of every part of the flora, including roots, barks, petals, flowers, resins, and even twigs. Isn't nature simply amazing? Just by extracting these basic plant parts alone, you will be able to derive wonderfully pleasant scents and natural aromas to infuse into your candles and rejuvenate your home.

MORE ON ESSENTIAL OILS

Because fragrance oils are synthetic, a more natural alternative to scenting your candles is to use essential oils. However, because essential oils are natural and don't have any artificial ingredients, they will evaporate prematurely if you do not add them at the precise moment to your candles. The right moment to add essential oils is when your melted wax begins the cooling down process—be careful not to wait until the wax solidifies, or your essential oils won't be able to blend well with the candle.

What you need to do is to melt the wax at the ideal temperature of between 122 and 180 degrees Fahrenheit (50 – 80 Celsius). Remember that each kind of essential oil has its own flash point, which is the temperature at which the oil will catch fire and burn up.

To keep candle making at home as safe as possible, you need to be aware of the varying flash points of every essential oil.

Generally, this flash point is above the soy wax's melting temperature. Keep in mind that if you add the oil below the flash point, you will be able to preserve the scent well, so it's best to go for essential oils with high flash points to keep those powerful scents intact.

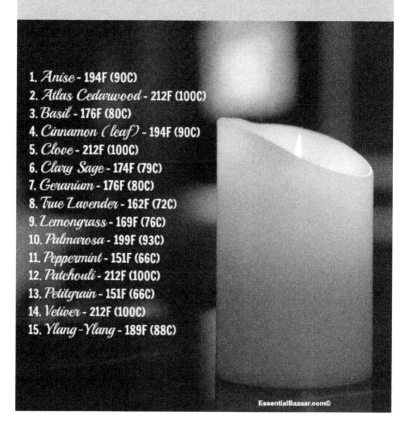

Soy Candle Making

Flashpoints of Essential Oils

1. Anise - 194F (90C)
2. Atlas Cedarwood - 212F (100C)
3. Basil - 176F (80C)
4. Cinnamon (leaf) - 194F (90C)
5. Clove - 212F (100C)
6. Clary Sage - 174F (79C)
7. Geranium - 176F (80C)
8. True Lavender - 162F (72C)
9. Lemongrass - 169F (76C)
10. Palmarosa - 199F (93C)
11. Peppermint - 151F (66C)
12. Patchouli - 212F (100C)
13. Petitgrain - 151F (66C)
14. Vetiver - 212F (100C)
15. Ylang-Ylang - 189F (88C)

EssentialBazaar.com©

Image source:
https://i2.wp.com/www.essentialbazaar.com/wp-content/uploads/2016/05/Essential-Oil-Flashpoints.jpg?w=830&ssl=1

15 ESSENTIAL OILS YOU CAN USE IN CANDLEMAKING

- ➢ Star anise – Similar to black licorice, the scent of the anise essential oil has a sweet and rich note, which helps treat colds, bronchitis, and the flu.
- ➢ Basil essential oil – This top note essential oil has a sweet and herbaceous scent which helps fight viral infections and various inflammations.

- ➢ Atlas Cedarwood essential oil – The woody fragrance of this essential oil is balanced well with some sweetness as a wonderful base note, and can relieve arthritis symptoms, coughing, and bronchitis. It is a natural option for stress relief and can ease tension as well as energize the body.

- ➢ Cinnamon essential oil (leaf) – This essential oil is a common favorite in soy candle making for its sweet and spicy fragrance that also doubles as an aphrodisiac and a salve for the mind and body.

- ➢ Clove essential oil – Invigorating and rejuvenating, the clove essential oil has a spicy fragrance that serves as an aphrodisiac and a great body stimulant as well.

- Clary Sage essential oil – The earthy and fruity scent of this middle note, when diffused, helps relieve tension and aches from menstrual pain and coughing fits.

- Geranium essential oil – Floral and fresh, geranium essential oil can invigorate and uplift the mind and spirit, as well as cleanse the unpurified air.

- True Lavender essential oil – As one of the most popular essential oils, lavender relaxes the nervous system of the body and promotes relaxation and good sleep. It helps ease anxieties and provides peace of mind for stressful individuals.

- Lemongrass essential oil – The lemony scent of the lemongrass essential oil calms down gastrointestinal issues, digestive upsets, and flatulence. It is also said to repel pesky mosquitoes and keep insects at bay.

- Palmarosa essential oil – Used for air purification, the floral and sweet scent of the Palmarosa essential oil can also help boost weakened immune systems and relieve respiratory issues.

- Peppermint essential oil – The strong minty scent of the peppermint essential oil also makes it a favorite among candle makers. It not only helps energize the body and stimulate the mind, but it can also help ease fatigue, relieve sinusitis, and help with a migraine and nausea.

- ➢ Patchouli essential oil – Patchouli is an aphrodisiac that eases nerves and stimulates the vital processes of the body.

- ➢ Petitgrain essential oil – The petitgrain's citrusy scent makes it a great partner for citrus oils to uplift the spirit and energize the body.

- ➢ Vetiver essential oil – This smoky base note is strong and has a herbaceous scent that can help calm nerves, relieve muscle pain, and ease anxieties.

- ➢ Ylang-Ylang essential oil – Rich and oriental in its fragrance, the Ylang-Ylang is well-known for the joyous and stress-relieving effect that it brings to any home.

With essential oils, you can also create your own blends and mix and match the oils for the perfect scent that suits your own tastes.

Whatever combination you decide to create, you can be sure that the essential oils can stimulate the mind as a tonic, energize the body, and help you sleep better.

Essential oils can calm you down, de-stress you when you are feeling too overwhelmed with the daily grind of everyday life, and help ease migraines and body pains. The antibacterial, anti-fungal, and anti-inflammatory properties of essential oils can not only improve your symptoms but can also promote good memory and help purify the air too!

A few self-made blends include lemongrass with geranium, cinnamon and clove, spruce and pine oil. You can also add patchouli to any other essential oil for an earthy note, as well as mix in orange for long-lasting fragrances and Ylang-Ylang to smoothen out any blend.

5 MUST FOLLOW STEPS TO CREATE YOUR ESSENTIAL OIL CANDLES

- Pour in 450g of your soy wax flakes into your chosen container. Just in case the wax rises after melting, leave some space at the top.

- Then, place your container inside your oven. Heat it for about 30 seconds, pausing to take regular breaks, for 3 minutes. Whenever you take a break from heating, remember to use a wooden spoon to stir the wax to make sure that the heat spreads evenly so that the wax will be able to melt properly.

- Remove the container from the oven after 3 minutes, and with your wooden spoon, mix your drops of essential oils into the wax. Just remember that the more drops of essential oils you put in, the stronger the scent will be, so how much to mix in is completely up to you.

- Now, with a wooden skewer, hold the candle in place in the mason jar and wrap the wick around the skewer. Wrap this about three times and drop the wick into your chosen container.

- Make sure that the wick is at the center of the glass by taping it down to the bottom to make it stay in its place. You can now pour in your wax, remembering to hold the wick in place until your wax hardens upright. You can let this harden in the fridge for about 2 hours, and trim the wick as needed, usually about an inch. And that's it!

TROUBLESHOOTING COMMON CANDLE MAKING PROBLEMS AND ISSUES

Now, nobody is perfect, and practicing constantly is the only way you will ever achieve perfection in your candle making business. Because you are just starting out, you will undoubtedly encounter a variety of problems and issues on your first foray into this wonderful adventure, but fret not!

I've got some troubleshooting tips for you too as you embark on this journey, so chin up, puff up your chest, and get confident! I am absolutely positive that you can do this!

CANDLE APPEARANCE

SURFACE CRACKS IN YOUR CANDLES

When you have cracks in the surface of your candle, this is probably due to the fact that you cooled your candle too quickly. To remedy this, you can try to heat your mold properly before you pour in your wax, just so it can cool down more slowly and properly.

If for instance, you are using a water bath to cool your candle down, you can opt to use a water bath that is slightly warmer. Always remember that you should never use a freezer to cool down your candle as this will almost always give you surface cracks in your candle.

YOU GET BUBBLE IN THE SURFACE OF YOUR CANDLE

Pits or bubbles form in the surface of your candle when your candle is cooled to fast as well. Cooling your candle too quickly allows the air bubbles to escape, causing those annoying surface pits.

To solve this issue, you can also try to heat your mold before you pour your wax in. You can use a heat gun or a blow dryer to heat your mold first, or you may want to use a higher temperature when you are heating your wax.

You can also use a warm water bath to make sure that you candle surface is nice and smooth.

THERE IS A DULL SURFACE IN YOUR CANDLE

To keep your candle surface from being dull, you can use a piece of nylon stocking to buff your candle surface and give it a particularly attractive shine.

YOUR CANDLE CONTAINER FORMS SOME WET SPOTS

Wet spots on your container candles can occur when your wax pulls away from the container of your candle. You can choose to heat your container first before you pour in your wax, or add some vybar to the wax (just about a quarter teaspoon per pound will be good enough).

CANDLE BURNING

YOUR CANDLE COLLAPSES

With pillar candles, every now and then, you might encounter the problem of your candle collapsing. When there are huge air bubbles inside your candles, your pillar candle might just collapse.

To prevent this, you can poke some relief holes around your wick as it cools. This will keep those air bubbles from forming.

THERE IS EXCESS WAX

As your wax burns, there might be some excess wax on the sides of your container. To keep this from happening, you need to use a wick that's not too small for your chosen container. Pick one that's a bit larger instead. Also, you might want to try to burn your candles for at least about an hour for every diameter inch of your candle.

As excess wax can occur when you burn your candle for too short of a duration, you need to burn your candles at the right duration of time in every sitting. When your candle burns straight down the middle, this phenomenon can happen when your wick is too small as well.

YOUR WICK IS SMOKING

Remember to trim your wick to about a quarter of an inch before you burn your candle to keep your wick from smoking. Place your candle in a room with no drafts, and make sure that your wick is not too large.

LARGE FLAME AND SMALL FLAME

If you flame is too large, your wick is too big for your candle. If your flame is too small, on the other hand, your wick may be too small for your candle as well, or your colorants and essential oils might be clogging up your wick. There is such a thing as mixing too many additives, so be sure not to let these fragrances and colorants choke your wick.

THE WICK DOES NOT STAY LIT

The melting wax may drown out your wick, and this happens when your wick is too small. Go for a larger wick to prevent it from having difficulty staying lit up.

MISCELLANEOUS PROBLEMS AND ISSUES

THE CANDLE GETS STUCK IN THE MOLD

When you are choosing the best mold to use and before you even start making your candles, pick a mold that is free of melted wax and has no dents. You can use some silicone spray or vegetable oil and spray it into your mold before pouring in your wax.

You can also try to place your candle in the freezer for about 10 minutes to shrink it and have it pop out easily—just don't leave it in the freezer for too long if you don't want to have cracks on the surface of your candle.

THE FRAGRANCE OR SCENT IS NOT STRONG ENOUGH

Before you begin, it is important to remember that scents have different properties and the scent throw happens when your candle burns for about 2 or 3 hours with the candle top melted. If your scent is still weak despite all those factors, you might want to consider adding in a bit more when you drop your fragrances in during your candle making process. Different brands also have different properties, so always try to experiment with your scents.

If the fragrance that you added to the melted wax was less than 10%, then you definitely need to add more drops. You should also check the flash point of your fragrance oil because adding the oil at a temperature above its flash point evaporates the oil right out of the candle even before it has had the chance to set in.

Lastly, keep in mind that the larger the melt pool, the more scent is given off. Always make sure that your candle has a large melt pool as it burns.

THE CANDLE KEEPS TUNNELING

To keep your candle from tunneling, you can try to increase your wick size. You might also want to try double wicking if you have a container that is big enough for that. Despite this, if you put out the candle even before it has had the chance to melt to its sides, this can cause some tunneling as well even if you use the wick with the correct size, so you need to avoid that too.

Random Tips and Tricks

Research, research, research.

Before you even begin to build your candle making empire, it's important first to determine what your goals are and what you want to accomplish. Planning ahead is key to everything, and this can make or break your lucrative endeavor.

You should first know and decide what wax you want to use. What are the varying types of waxes? What type of wick do you want to use? Do you want to use additives as well? Afterward, you should determine what type of containers you want to use. Some may be easier to use than others, while some have particular ways of usage and have different pros and cons. Irregularly shaped jars, for example, can be a challenge to the wick.

It is also crucial for you to keep testing your candles. Testing means you need to burn your candle for a specific duration and then record and document the performance of that candle. Take note of the melt pool, flame height, scent throw, wick characteristics, and other helpful notes.

It's always great to be optimistic and to think that you will be able to master the art of candle making as quickly and as efficiently as possible right away, but the truth is that there are some things that will always go wrong, and the best thing you can do to prepare for such starting slip-ups is to buy supplies in smaller batches at first.

By buying packs that come in 1 lb to 5 lb quantities, you can try out some recipes and create testing batches first without having to waste whole packs once opened. Usually, a pound of wax is enough to make a candle or two. You can also buy sampler sets of wicks, or wicks that come in packs of 5 or 10.

Be careful not to jump the gun when buying fragrance oils as well. If everything starts to become too overwhelming for you, try to buy starter kits first, at least until you get the hang of what you are doing. You can check Artfire.com, Etsy.com, eBay, flea markets, and even local yard sales.

You should also keep in mind that it is best to buy supplies from suppliers who are easily accessible and are local to where you are. In the unfortunate event that you run into a candle supply emergency, you at least know that you will not need to venture out too far just to get the supplies you need.

BONUS MATERIAL - ATTRACTIVE PACKAGING THAT SELLS MORE

They say that marketing is everything and that sometimes, no matter how good your product is, it just cannot simply speak for itself without good publicity and branding. This is where attractive packaging comes in. When your containers and packages are pleasing to the eye and visually stimulating, you can bet that your customers will immediately be compelled to buy your products just because they look amazing and fabulous.

Plus, with great packaging, you can also boost your sales when it comes to the holiday season, on birthdays, or any other celebratory occasion, because beautiful packaging makes for a great gift item.

Candles, of course, have always been a favorite of gift-givers, and you will definitely want to take advantage of that huge market.

The wonderful thing about candle packaging is that you can always make use of the candle's natural color as part of the attractiveness of the packaging itself. With great packaging, you can show off your candle's pretty shade and highlight its color combinations. This is the perfect opportunity to grab a huge chunk of the market share for home decorations as well, as colorful candles in pretty packages can have a colossal impact on buyers who want to decorate and beautify their homes.

So how exactly do you add flair and personality to your candle's packaging?

Here is a Bing.com search page that shows various attractive packaging ideas including the seven I talk about below.

http://www.bing.com/images/search?sp=2&pq=candle+pac kaging&sk=IM1&sc=8-16&cvid=A2E21F0464364704BDBFAED51F255822&q=cand le+packaging+ideas&qft=&FORM=IRFLTR

7 CREATIVE CANDLE PACKAGING IDEAS

CARDBOARD BOX

Plain and thin cardboard boxes may not look much, but when you think about simplicity, they can be a great candle packaging idea. Because they come in varying shapes and sizes, you can pretty much always find one that best fits your candle of choice.

They also come in different colors, so you can mix and match the colors of the boxes to the colors of your candles.

You can place some bubble wrap or packing peanuts inside the box before you place your fragile candle, and then simply slap on a sticker or a stamp of your logo in front. It can be your company, your candle "flavor," your candle's statistics and features, your website, some safety precautions when lighting up the candle, or even some ideas on how to properly enjoy the candle at home.

As the perfect icing on the cake, you can tie a ribbon or a charming décor around the box as a finishing touch.

DIY AND SELF-MADE PACKAGING

With this option, you can save some time and resources if you make your candle's container the packaging in itself. Pour the wax directly into your decorative jar, aluminum tin, Mason jar, or glass jar—just be sure not to burn yourself while doing it!

Look for glass jars and containers that are specifically made for candles to be on the safe side.

Then, you can design your logo or branding with a sticker, print them out, and stick them on the jar itself. You can also place the stickers and labels on the cover or on the tin on top, including some burning instructions and safety precautions. Finally, you can amp up the festivity by tying a bow around the candle.

FOOD IMITATION PACKAGING

The incredibly fun thing about making candles is that there's no end to the possibilities of the candle's shape and size. You can shape your candle to look and smell like food too! Candles can resemble packaged food, fruits, veggies, and other what-have-yous.

Depending on your chosen "food candle" of choice, you can design a packaging that matches the food that your candle is imitating.

For instance, if you have a candle that is shaped like some doughnuts or other baked goods, you can design a doughnut box and slap on your logo on the front. You can even create plastic or wood containers to make the candles look like they are being served on a food tray, or even on some dainty wicker baskets. Go ahead—get creative, let your imagination run wild, and have fun!

CLEAR BAGS

If you are going for efficiency and simplicity, you can always go for the most common packaging of all—the clear plastic bag. These inexpensive packages need not be boring and mundane—you can always spice things up by closing the clear polypropylene bags from packaging supply companies with some rope, raffia, ribbons, or twist ties.

This saves you a great deal of time and effort if you are at a particularly busy craft fair, where customers come in droves, and you might not have enough time to painstakingly package every single candle, especially if you are a one-man or one-woman team.

USEFUL OBJECTS AND OTHER RECYCLED HOME MATERIALS

People always use parchment paper and different types of wrapping paper to package gifts, and you can set yourself apart from the rest by using household items that your customers can reuse once the candle is used up. Who wouldn't' want to buy a candle and a mug at the same time?

This kind of philosophy will even encourage your customers and buyers to help save the environment by reducing wastage and recycling their household objects.

For example, you can package your candles well inside water bottles with wide mouth rims, painted bottles with fiery designs, and even coffee mugs and flower pots.

This way, when the candle is used up and gone, what will be left is the mug or pot that you've placed it in, making it completely reusable.

CREATIVE YET INFORMATIVE LABELS

Making labels might seem like a simple task, but just because they're just plain text, it doesn't mean that they have to be uninteresting. You can experiment and have fun with your varying designs!

The marketing trick is to make the product more appealing, but you also have to make sure that you include all the pertinent information on the label for your customers. Do you have some alerts and warnings about the dangers of candle fire?

Do you have some safety procedures when lighting the candle? Is it safe for children? What is the flavor, scent, and what are the ingredients you used to make the candle? Are there any hazards that the buyer should know about? What is the net content of the candle?

These are the facts that you always have to include on your labels for your customer. This not only keeps them safe, but it also reassures them that you are a reputable and trustworthy seller and manufacturer and that you will always have their safety and best interests at heart despite being a seller.

Remember, in this cut-throat industry of candle making, one of the great things that will set you apart is your own personal touch and the care and concern that you personally give to each and every one of your buyers. They will know that you have put your whole heart into this endeavor, and they will likely buy from you more and become your loyal repeat customers because of that.

HERBAL EMBEDDED CANDLE PACKAGING

Here is a wonderfully unique idea to package your candle without really packaging them in anything. You can create an herbal design for your candle, all while being green, natural, and chemical-free!

Because herbal leaf shapes and flowers already naturally form a great wealth of decorating possibilities, you can use herbs to stick in or around your candles in plenty of fun and exciting ways. And the best part of it all is that when you are done experimenting with your herbs, and you are not satisfied or happy with your outcome, you can always melt the wax back down, strain it, and start all over again!

In order to embed a dried leaf or a sprig inside your candle, you need to prevent mildew by using only the dried material. Dry up those herbs by popping them inside the microwave for a few seconds, and when you embed them into the candle, they will show through the wax with beautiful and unique effects. Place these dried herbs and leaves near the surface but not too close to the wick to prevent them from catching fire.

First, pour your melted wax into your mold and wait until the outside has set, approximately to about 1/8 thick. Then, pour your liquid wax back into the container, and leave a shell of hardened wax. You can then position your herbs the way you want to, then use a knife or ice pick to cut chunks and pile them against the herbs to hold them in position.

The leaves or the flowers that you want to emboss need to be pressed and dried, perhaps with a thick phone book and such, for a few days. You can use some glue or hot wax to position the pressed leaves on the candle surface until the glue dries of the wax hardens.

Make sure that they are firmly held in place, then coat your creative design with a thin layer of wax. This will help hold the herbs in place and keep them from being broken or scratched off. You can also hold your candle by its wick and dip the entire candle in melted wax for a few seconds.

3 Branding samples and ideas

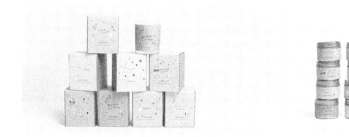

Some packages tell a continuous story, like when you put all boxes together in a straight line and form a whole image across the side. Some use stamps instead to give off an earthy homemade vibe.

Now that we have discussed the different ideas that you can use to create your own flavor and put your own spin into your creative packaging, let's take a look at some creative examples of different brands, shall we?

BON LUX

The distinctive design element of this Bon Lux brand here is that the company used hand-drawn illustrations to portray the ambiance and feel of every candle. You do not really have to be a huge company or a well-oiled machine to create these branding labels and packages.

All you need to do is to print your labels on a separate paper. You can use pastel colors and keep a quirky vibe with some illustrations as well.

THE CANDLE GIRL

Here, the brand is distinct in itself because of its use of a marble candle. It can be quirky, or it can exude an aura of sophistication and elegance depending on the perception you want to portray. With a marble texture and color in the candle, you can set yourself apart from all the other plain colored candles out there.

REWINED CANDLES & LABORATORY PERFUMES

Most candle packages are limited to boxes and cardboard, but with this brand, it makes use of the candle's natural form and creates cylinders and bags.

This unique medium takes advantage of the candle's cylindrical form without looking too common—and at the same time, the cloth bag can also be reused if needed.

Image source:

https://craftycandlesupplies.com.au/media/wy

siwyg/Blog/Rewined-and-Lab-Final-2.jpg

With these examples and concepts in mind, always remember that your packaging should be a creative extension of your branding.

It should reflect the perception and the value of your product, as well as make you stand out from the crowd. Do not be afraid to think outside the box—by not using a box!

FINAL TIPS

By now, you should already be a candle making master, and are probably ready to head out into the world and share your creative gifts with your family, friends, neighbors, and community. Before you do, let me give you a proper send-off by sharing some final words and tips on your candles.

When you are shopping for new candles and wicks, make sure that you look for lead-free labels and statements that tell you just how safe your candle ingredients and materials are. When you have candles that haven't been burned yet, try to rub the tip of the wick on a piece of paper.

Watch out if it leaves a gray pencil-like mark because this means that your wick contains a lead core. Candles with metal core wicks need to be disposed of as a precaution, or you can ask for a refund from your supplier.

Just to be on the safe side, here are some of the good brands you can rely on when you are purchasing your candles for further reference:

- Way Out Wax – With candles that are made from a hundred percent beeswax, this company from Morrisville, Vermont also uses a combination of vegetable wax and hemp oil wax, so you can be sure that you are using natural ingredients with the candles. Cotton or hemp is the material used for the wick, and essential plant oils are used for their fragrances. Here's a handy-dandy tip in order to minimize soot: trim your wicks to about a quarter of an inch, and also, do not burn your candles against a draft.

- Ava – Organic coconut wax, organic beeswax, natural cotton wicks, and pure essential oils— how else can you go wrong?

- Big Dipper Wax Works – Big Dipper Wax Works also uses a hundred percent beeswax in their candles, and best of all, their candles come in varying shapes and sizes, with pillars, votives, tapers, tea lights, and quirky molds like hearts and stars.

- EmzBlendz – Is there anything even better than candles that you can reuse? With EmzBlendz, their pure soy wax candles come in glass jars that are travel-friendly. They come in a wide variety of scents such as cranberry spice, coconut lime, or even lemongrass sage for the perfect relaxation and aromatherapy—even inside your bathroom.

- BeSem Natural Scents — When the company name itself means "pure, natural, a sweet smell" in Hebrew, you can be sure you are getting the real thing. These homemade candles come in Mason jars and can be quite handy—not to mention you can also reuse those Mason jars after the candle has been used up completely.

- Honey Candles — Once again, Honey Candles, from the name itself, produces a hundred percent pure beeswax candles to not only purify the air inside your home sans the toxins, but also provide for a warm, cozy, and homey glow with a honey scent. The company also supports the Foundation for the Preservation of Honey Bees, so you know that you are giving back to the community with every candle purchase.

- Sunbeam Candles, Inc. — Speaking of giving back and helping preserve the environment, you can also help Mother Earth with Sunbeam Candles because the company uses solar power to hand-craft their candles. They also use beeswax, soy wax and aromatherapy candles, and they ship carbon-neutral as well as are a certified living wage employer. Talk about being a friend for all!

You can go ahead and purchase from these eco-friendly and natural brands to get an idea of what you want to do, what you want to accomplish, and how to achieve them.

These brands can be inspirations for you, samples for your experiments, or simply just a way for you to help fellow natural candle makers out there—after all, we are all in the same boat here!

LAST WORDS

So, now that you are fully equipped and ready to go why not get started with your very first candle batch? And once you're a natural candle making empire, drop me a line, would you? I would definitely love to hear from you and talk more about this beautiful shared passion we have!

I want to say THANK YOU for purchasing and reading this book. I really hope you got a lot out of it!

Can I ask you for a quick favor though?

If you enjoyed this book, I would really appreciate it if you could leave me a Review on Amazon.

I LOVE getting feedback from my wonderful readers, and reviews on Amazon really do make the difference. I read all of my reviews and would love to hear your thoughts. If you need to contact me for any reason, please feel free to email at rolpublishing@gmail.com

Thank you so much!!

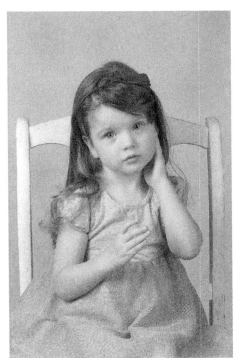

REFERENCES

http://www.candlewic.com/service/about-candlewic/the-history-of-candles-and-candlemaking/page.aspx?id=2216

https://www.everythingdawnbakerycandles.com/blogs/news/34785665-the-pros-and-cons-of-soy-wax

https://www.benefits-of-honey.com/beeswax-candles.html

https://www.fragrancex.com/fragrance-information/a-candle-making.html

https://craftycandlesupplies.com.au/wick_guide_choosing_the_best_wicks_for_your_soy_candles/

https://craftycandlesupplies.com.au/media/wysiwyg/Guides/Dye-guide/Liquid-Dye.jpg

http://www.candlewic.com/newsletter/2015-en-light-eners/crazy-for-candle-color/page.aspx?id=2356

http://presentitude.com/wp-content/uploads/2015/09/10901ColorWheel.png

http://www.bathalchemylab.com/2010/05/natural-candles-coloring-your-candles.html

https://www.essentialbazaar.com/how-to-make-fragrance-oils-for-candles-faq-and-recipes/

https://www.motherearthliving.com/garden-projects/light-up-your-life

https://i2.wp.com/www.essentialbazaar.com/wp-content/uploads/2016/05/Essential-Oil-Flashpoints.jpg?w=830&ssl=1

https://www.candlescience.com

http://www.crafterstouch.com/tip.aspx?tipid=33

https://craftycandlesupplies.com.au/blog/Candle_packaging_inspiration/

https://craftycandlesupplies.com.au/media/wysiwyg/Blog/Bon-Lux-Final-2.jpg

https://craftycandlesupplies.com.au/media/wysiwyg/Blog/Candle-Girl-Final-2.jpg

https://craftycandlesupplies.com.au/media/wysiwyg/Blog/Rewined-and-Lab-Final-2.jpg

http://www.care2.com/greenliving/7-candles-that-wont-give-you-cancer-or-make-your-kids-sick.html

Printed in Great Britain
by Amazon